THE BENEFITS OF THE CROSS OF JESUS

Annette Stanley

Watkins Christian Publishing

Contents

THE BENEFITS OF THE CROSS OF JESUS

How can we appropriate the benefits of The Cross? By Faith. There are no substitutions for living by faith. We must trust in God's character and believe He is righteous, just, faithful, and will keep all His promises. The Cross is a trinitarian event; God the Father, Son, and Holy Ghost possess a single will. When we understand the revelation of the complete and perfect work of the Cross, we can begin receiving all its benefits, including God's supernatural power.

In the book of Ephesians 2:8-9, For by grace you have been saved through faith; and this is not your own doing, it is the gift of God, not a result of works, so that no one may boast.

What does the bible say about faith? Hebrews 11:1, Now faith is the substance of things hoped for, the evidence of things not seen. This involves trusting God in all circumstances, which enables the believer to remain loyal to God and His word. Faith takes God at His word and relies entirely on His promises. The confidence that comes with faith is based on the God who fulfills His promises. It means that, in our various circumstances, we live out our belief "that God exists and that He rewards those who sincerely seek Him." Those who live by faith take confident action based on what God has revealed about His character, seeking to do His will in all things. Our faith itself is the evidence of the reality of what we hope for. Faith is a requirement for receiving God's gift of spiritual salvation. Faith involves repentance (i.e., admitting, expressing genuine sorrow for, and turning from our sinful, God-defying way) and a complete turning toward God to follow Christ. Faith also includes obedience to Jesus Christ and His Word. Such obedience must become a way of life, inspired by our trust in Christ, our gratitude to God, and the life-transforming work of the Holy Spirit; it is an "obedience to faith." for this reason, faith and obedience go together. Faith was released from the Cross.

WHAT IS MERCY?

Compassion or forgiveness is shown toward someone whom it is within one's power to punish or harm, an event to be grateful for, especially because its occurrence prevents something unpleasant or provides relief from suffering. Jesus did exactly this for the entire human race, and He gave us Mercy! Mercy could be described as God sparing us from the consequences and judgment we deserve. But God, who is rich in mercy, for His great love wherewith He loved us even when we were dead in sins hath quickened us together with Christ. Mercy triumphs over judgment.

Lamentations 3:22-23 It is of the Lord's mercies that we are not consumed because His compassions fail not. They are new every morning; great is thy faithfulness. Mercy was released from the cross.

WHAT IS GRACE?

It is an undeserved gift; it is God's eternal presence, full of power, that gives us the ability to be and to do everything we cannot accomplish in our strength. Grace could be described as God granting us favors and benefits we do not deserve. When we act without God's grace, we become a legalistic Christian. Legalism is the human effort of trying to please God based on one's merit. It attempts to become holy and righteous through rules, traditions, and laws. No measure of validation on earth could ever amount to the security of being chosen by God. He lavished His glorious grace over us through the high price of Jesus' blood, a currency beyond our comprehension. God wants us to believe and receive since we are justified by faith in Jesus and His redeeming work at the Cross. Grace was released from the Cross.

The most significant unseen reality we must each discover to live the life we were meant to be the spiritual reality of our supernatural God. The Cross of Jesus is the only legal and legitimate source that can open the door of

God's supernatural realm to us. If God had intended for humanity to remain only in the natural realm, He never would have provided a way through His Son Jesus on the Cross for us to be restored to a relationship with Him, nor given us access to Himself and His supernatural power through faith. Acts 17:24-25, He is the God who made the world and everything in it. Since He is Lord of heaven and earth, He doesn't live in man-made temples, and human hands can't serve His needs, for He has no need.

He gives life and breath to everything and satisfies every need. Apostle Paul also writes, for in Him we live and move and have our being. Forasmuch then as we are the offspring of God, we ought not to think that the Godhead is like unto gold, silver, or stone, graven by art and man's device. And the times of this ignorance God winked at; but now commandeth all men everywhere to repent because He hath appointed a day, in the which He will judge the world in righteousness by that man (Jesus) whom He hath ordained; whereof He hath given assurance unto all men, in that He hath raised Him from the dead. So, you see, without the Cross of Jesus Christ, humanity would be lost and without hope.

Some examples of false gods: Budda did not go to the Cross, Muhammad did not go to the Cross, or any other false gods such as Ashtoreth (goddess of the Canaanites), Chemosh (god of the Moabites), Dagon (god of the Philistines), Marduk (god of the Babylonians) even the modern-day David Koresh (who became the leader of the core group of Branch Davidians) claimed to be the son of God, the Christ for the last days and the Lamb of Revelation. But, according to the Bible, which is the Word of God, Jesus Christ, the Son of the Living God, is the only one who went to the Cross as the Savior. These false gods that are in the Bible could not talk, walk, heal, deliver, or breathe life into man or anything else because they were made by man's hands, carved out of gold, stone, and wood. God is the God of all creation; he is revealed in the Bible as an infinite, eternal, self-existent—without beginning or ending, who is the "First Cause," the Original Source, Initiator, and Creator of all that is. A simpler way to think of this reality is that there has never been a moment when God did not exist. As Moses testifies in Psalm 90:2, Before the mountains were brought forth, or ever thou hadst formed the earth and the world, even from everlasting to everlasting, thou art GOD. Moses is saying that God existed eternally, forever and infinitely, without beginning or end. God is independent of and existed before all that was created in heaven and on earth. So, God is the life giver; And the LORD GOD formed man of the dust of the ground and breathed into his nostrils the breath of life, and man became a living soul (Genesis 2:7).

WHAT IS SALVATION?

S alvation is deliverance from sin and its consequences, which Christians believe is brought about by faith in Christ Jesus; preservation or deliverance from harm, ruin, or loss; a source or means of being saved from harm, ruin, or loss. In simpler terms, it means being saved from eternal damnation and living in eternity with God the Father.

The very nature of the word salvation means there are some threatening or deadly conditions from which we must be rescued. According to the bible, this points to being delivered from the consequences of sin and the clutches of death and Satan. The major theme of deliverance in the New Testament is deliverance from God's wrath. In 1st Thessalonians 1:10, Apostle Paul is addressing the Thessalonians and their faith in God, how they are looking forward to the coming of Jesus, and how He has rescued them from the terrors of the coming judgment. Romans 5:8-9 also speaks of us being delivered from the wrath to come. But God commended His love toward us in that Christ died for us while we were yet sinners. Much more then being now justified by His blood, we shall be saved from wrath through Him. The real problem is sin, but God sent His only begotten Son, Jesus Christ, to rescue us from sin and its deadly consequences. Everyone falls into the category of "sinner" Romans 3:23, for **all** have sinned and come short of the glory of God. It doesn't matter whether you are rich or poor, whether you're among the haves or have-nots, whether you live in the ghetto or a mansion in Beverly Hills; we **all** have sinned! So, unless something happens to change your condition, you're on your way to eternal hell; Jesus has changed your condition, hallelujah, glory to God.

What are we saved to?

All who receive "The Son" of God are saved to eternal life with God. The gospel of Jesus Christ brings life to all who receive Him! It brings us to the Almighty God Himself, and we were brought into a relationship with God and have everlasting life in eternity with Him. Salvation brings us to peace with God. Romans 5:1, therefore being justified by faith, we have peace with God through our Lord Jesus Christ. We are brought into freedom through Christ. John 8:36, if the Son therefore shall make you free, ye shall be free indeed.

In Acts 16:30-31, a Philippian jailer asks a very important question. Sirs, what must I do to be saved? The Apostles did not hesitate to point him to Jesus Christ as the only means by which men would be saved.

In 1ˢᵗTimothy 1:15, this is a faithful saying and worthy of all acceptations, that Christ Jesus came into the world to save sinners; this is very clear why the scripture said in John 14:6 that Jesus is the way, the truth, and the life, no man cometh unto the Father, but by Him. John 3:16-17, For God so loved the world, that He gave His only begotten Son, that whosoever believeth in Him should not perish but have everlasting life. For God sent not His Son into the world to condemn the world; but that the world through Him might be saved.

The crucifixion and resurrection of Jesus Christ are the two most important events for Christians. Those who have true faith in Christ should consider themselves united with Him in such a way that they relate to and identify with Him in His death and resurrection. In a sense, all Christians have been crucified with Christ on the cross. In addition, Christians have been freed from the law's requirement of relying on imperfect sacrifices to receive forgiveness and maintain a relationship with God.

1) Galatians 2:20, I am crucified with Christ; nevertheless, I live; yet not I, but Christ liveth in me. And the life I now live in the flesh, I live by the faith of the Son of God, who loved me and gave himself for me.

2) Romans 6:5, For if we have been united with Him in a death like His, we will certainly also be united with Him in a resurrection like His (NIV version).

AT THE CROSS

The events at The Cross changed history and paid the wages of sin for all humanity, all ages, centuries, past, present, and future, including those who have yet to be born. Everything we need was provided by The Cross of Jesus Christ, whether mentally, physically, power, authority, love, peace, joy, and healing in your body; whatever you may be facing at this very moment, look to The Cross of Jesus Christ. All the countless messages that are preached, all the theological books that have been written; all of this is good in its place, but none of them will help us if we fail to appropriate "The Power of the Cross," no religion in the world can equal the message of The Cross of Jesus Christ. When we stop placing the "Cross" at the center of our message, our faith loses its meaning, and we end up in bondage to traditions, regulations, and laws that are impossible to obey. The Lord said this to me in 2015: my people have become so familiar with the familiar until the familiar has put them in bondage. The Lord took me to His Word, Galatians 5:1: Stand fast therefore in the liberty wherewith Christ hath made us free, and be not entangled again with the yoke of bondage. If Jesus had not gone to the Cross, I dare to think, where would we be today because the Cross is not popular! The first Adam fell and stripped the entire human race of the righteousness of God; we needed a Savior! This is why God sent His Son, Jesus.

At the Cross, Jesus delivered us from the old man (2nd Corinthians 5:17); therefore, if any man is in Christ, he is a new creature; old things are passed away; behold, all things become new.

At the Cross, Jesus substituted himself for guilty sinners. He put Himself in our place, and we were bought with a price: therefore, glorify God in your body and in your spirit, which is God's (1st Corinthians 6:20).

At the Cross, Jesus took on our curse. Christ redeemed us from the curse of the law by becoming a curse for us. For it is written, "cursed" is everyone who is hanged on a tree (Galatians 3:13). He carried our curse so that we could be blessed.

At the Cross, Jesus clothed us, Mark 15:24, And when they had crucified Him, they parted his garments among them, casting lots for them to decide what each should take. This also fulfills a prophecy found in Psalm 22:18 they part my garments among them and cast lots upon my vesture. Ironically, they didn't recognize that through "The Cross," Jesus would be clothing His people! The prophet Isaiah wrote, I will greatly rejoice in the Lord, my soul shall be joyful in my God; for He hath clothed me with the garments of salvation, He hath covered me with the robe of righteousness (Isaiah 61:10).

At the Cross, Jesus tore open heaven for you. The tearing of the "veil of the temple" signified that a way was open into the presence of God. The curtain separating the Holy Place from the Most Holy Place represented sinful humanity's separation from a Holy God. Access was restricted to all except the high priest and then only under strict conditions at the appointed time. Thank God for Jesus. He filled the role of the ultimate high priest with full access to God the Father and opened permanent access to God for all those who surrender their lives to Him.

At the Cross, when Jesus said, "IT IS FINISHED," "My God, it was not a cry of defeat but a shout of triumph, declaring the completion of His work on the Cross! This triumph declaration was a signal that Jesus had fulfilled His earthly mission given by the Father. He fulfilled the Old Testament prophecy about the Messiah's suffering, He completed the work of spiritual rescue and restoration by providing the perfect sacrifice for sin, He secured the decisive victory over Satan and his network of demons, and Jesus achieved the means of restoring God's relationship with His creation and sinful humanity. Absolutely nothing can be or needs to be added to Christ's finished work on the Cross, and the results are ongoing! Considering God's wonderful and creative acts, it may seem ironic that His highest purpose to bring eternal life came through death. The Creator (God) sacrificed His Son for His creation. At the beginning of this book, The Cross is a trinitarian event; God the Father, Son, and Holy Ghost possess a single will; this is all God.

At the Cross, Jesus shed His blood. Matthew 26:28, For this is my blood of the New Testament, which is shed for many for the remission of sins.

The Cross redeemed and forgave us. Colossians 1:14, In whom we have redemption through His blood, even the forgiveness of sins. The Cross brings peace and reconciliation and unity, Colossians 1:20, And having made peace through the blood of his Cross, by Him to reconcile all things unto Himself. In a biblical sense, "to reconcile" means to be restored to a right relationship with God. When Christ went to the Cross, He tore down the wall of partition that separated people of all nations who were not Israelites or Jewish and brought into unity people of all nations and backgrounds as they sought a personal relationship with him. Ephesians 4:5-6, There is one body, and one Spirit, even as ye are called in one hope of your calling; one Lord, one faith, one baptism, one God and Father of all, who is above all. And through all, and in you all.

THE POWER THAT BROKE SATAN'S BACK

Jesus canceled the record of the charges against us and took it away by nailing it to the "Cross." In this way, He disarmed the spiritual rulers and authorities, and He shamed them publicly by His victory over them on "The Cross" (Colossians 2:13-15)

The Cross gave us access to God. Having, therefore, brethren, boldness to enter the holiest by the blood of Jesus, by a new and living way, which He hath consecrated for us through the veil, that is to say, His flesh (Hebrews 10:19-20).

The Cross is Christ, God's power and wisdom, For the preaching of the cross, is to them that perish foolishness; but unto us which are saved, it is the power of God. For it is written, I will destroy the wisdom of the wise and will bring to nothing the understanding of the prudent (1st Corinthians 1:18-19).

The Cross was a "Divine Calling" on Jesus' Life; prophecy had to be fulfilled according to the Word of God. In the book of Hebrews chapter 10:7, the blood of animal sacrifices would never take away sins, but instead, those sacrifices reminded them of their sins year after year, and it wearied God. So, Jesus stepped out of heaven into human form; you have given me a body to offer, Lo, I come (in the volume of the book it is written of me) to do thy will, O God.

When the disciples looked at the cross, they saw everything shutting down, but when The Almighty God looked at the cross, He saw everything opening. When the disciples looked at the cross, they thought it was the end of everything and a major setback for them and all who believed in Jesus, but God saw a new beginning for everyone and a massive setup for everyone who called on the name of the Lord Jesus Christ. The Bible tells us in Romans 10:9-13 that if thou shalt confess with thy mouth the Lord Jesus and shalt believe in thine heart that God hath raised him from the dead, thou shalt be saved. For with the heart, man believeth unto righteousness, and with the mouth, confession is made unto salvation. For the scripture saith, whosoever believeth in him shall not be ashamed. For there is no difference between the Jew and the Greek: for the same LORD over all is rich unto all that call upon him. For whosoever shall call upon the name of the Lord shall be saved.

When the disciples looked at the cross, they could only see Jesus being crucified. When God looked at the cross, He saw Satan getting crushed. Genesis 3:14-15: And the LORD GOD said unto the serpent because thou hast done this, thou art cursed above all cattle, and above every beast of the field; upon thou belly shalt thou go and dust shalt thou eat all the days of thy life: and I will put enmity between thee and the woman and between thy seed and her seed; it shall bruise thy head, and thou shalt bruise his heel.

When the people looked at the cross, they saw a tomb. When God looked at the cross, He saw a womb. God took the womb of the tomb and supernaturally performed through His Son Jesus, His resurrecting power, and this power was "The Birthing of Our Salvation." John 11:25-26, Jesus said unto Martha, I am the resurrection and the life, he that believeth in me, though he were dead, yet shall he live; and whosoever liveth and believeth in me shall never die. When Jesus said, "I am the resurrection and the life," He was saying there is no resurrection apart from Him and no eternal life apart from Him. He does more than give life; He is Life, and therefore, death has no power over Him! Jesus proved that neither death nor the tomb was an obstacle to Him because neither one had dominion over Him. O death, where is thy sting? O grave, where is thy victory? Death has no dominion over those who are in Christ Jesus because they have entrusted their lives to

Him, so physical death is not a tragic end; it is instead the gateway to eternal life with God.

Jesus' death was deliberate; He did not die a victim; no one took His life; he voluntarily laid it down. Therefore, my Father loves me because I lay down my life, and I might take it again. No man taketh it from me, but I lay it down of myself. I have the power to lay it down, and I have the power to take it again—this commandment I received from my Father (John 10:17-18). As we can see, Jesus' death was his destiny, his purpose, and his assignment; because of this, all "The Benefits of The Cross" was released to humanity. Salvation is in store for all followers of Christ who are continually being made holy (i.e., morally pure, spiritually whole, separated from evil, and set apart for God's purposes) as they grow in their relationship with God.

We must keep ourselves in check and be reminded of how our Lord and Savior Jesus Christ went to his death on "The Cross" so that we can reap "The Benefits of The Cross." So, without the Cross, there would be no salvation; without the Cross, there would be no resurrection; without the Cross, we would still be dead in our sins and alienated from God.

John 10:10, We know the thief comes to steal, kill, and destroy; Jesus came that we might have life and life more abundantly! Hallelujah, Glory to God!

The Romans scourged Jesus before He went to the cross, not the Jews. The book of Deuteronomy 25:3 states that a criminal should not receive more than forty lashes. So, to avoid accidentally breaking this command, the Jews would only give a criminal 39 lashes. Apostle Paul mentioned this practice in 2nd Corinthians 11:24: "Five times I received from the Jews the forty lashes minus one." It is hard to imagine the level of hatred and punishment Jesus endured. Worse than this, the man they sent to be flogged and crucified was innocent, and He's the Son of God. The torment Jesus endured was prophesied in Isaiah: He was wounded for our transgressions, He was bruised for our iniquities, the chastisement of our peace was upon Him, and with His stripes we are healed (Isaiah 53:5). Can you imagine the pure, perfect innocence of Jesus Christ, His wisdom and power that He possessed in His human body, He could have at any time called legions of angels to come and protect Him for what He was facing? He was and is the flawless Shepherd who chose to accept an undeserved, cruel death to save His sheep, you and me. Before being arrested, Jesus prophesied His death. "I am the good Shepherd: the good Shepherd giveth His life for the sheep" (John 10:11).

When we go through our trials and tribulations, we sometimes see a tomb with our names written on it. My God, through the example of "The Cross," God takes the very thing(s) we thought was the end of our lives, the end of everything we hoped for, the end of what we believe Him for, the end of our dreams, but the Bible tells us, all things work together for good to them that love God, to them who are the called according to His purpose. I'm reminded of the scripture in the book of Ecclesiastes 7:8: Better is the end of a thing than the beginning thereof, and the patient in spirit is better than the proud in spirit. Solomon challenges us to keep pressing on toward our God-given goals no matter how difficult. We must recognize that God is working in us through all situations. We can rejoice in success and learn to trust God through adversity, knowing His promises. He takes all our situations and, by His redemptive grace, causes them to birth new possibilities through us for His Kingdom. He declared our end from the beginning of our lives. Jeremiah 29:11, For I know the thoughts that I think toward you, saith the LORD, thoughts of peace, and not of evil, to give you an expected end. Isaiah 55:8-9: For my thoughts, are not your thoughts; neither are your ways my ways, saith the LORD. For as the heavens are higher than the earth, so are my ways higher than your ways and my thoughts than your thoughts. We can rest in the Lord because God's word will never be canceled or void. His word will always accomplish its purposes by bringing spiritual life to those who receive it or judgment to those who reject it. Whatever you may be dealing with today, whether mental, emotional, physical, or guilt, the Cross of Jesus has the power to set you free.

Jesus is the perfect and innocent lamb taking on the sins of all men (not symbolically as in the Old Testament) when the priest would offer up an animal as a sacrifice for the sins of the people. The priest who was anointed would first lay hands upon the animal as a symbol of a transfer taking place (Leviticus 4:13-21). The people's sins were being transferred to the animal in the presence of the Lord, and the animal was being slain to symbolize that the payment for the moral price of sin, which is death, was paid. But Jesus offered up His sinless and "eternal being" as a sacrifice on the Cross to make moral payment for all sin, for all time.

The sacrifice had to be without sin to atone for sin; Jesus' divine nature makes His sacrifice good and valuable enough to exchange for all men because He is perfect and holy. His life is worth all other human life, so our sins were transferred to the Cross. When the Spirit of Jesus was released from the cross, forgiveness came from the cross, and guilty sinners were drawn by the Cross to receive forgiveness and eternal life with Jesus. Even though we cannot achieve perfection on this earth, the Cross of Jesus Christ will give us a hunger and thirst for it to help us live it. I believe no amount of self-discipline or willpower can make us love righteousness and live a holy life according to God's commandments; it only comes through The Power of the Cross and the Blood of Jesus Christ.

According to the Bible in Colossians 2:13-14, God erased the "handwriting of ordinances that was against us, which was contrary to us, and took it out of the way, nailing it to the Cross." Jesus' death obliterates the debt of sin, not the Law of Moses. The commandments exposed our offenses against God and our human inability to live up to God's perfect standards. This does not mean that God's laws and commands are obsolete. Romans 7:12, wherefore the law is holy and the commandments holy and just because they still expose sin and point people to their need for Christ today. The defeat of Satan by the Lord Jesus Christ is complete. He continues to defeat Satan today through the lives of the believers who have been delivered from the kingdom of darkness and transformed into the kingdom of light. When Christ returns, He will have Satan bound in the pit and then eventually thrown into the lake of fire. Revelation 20:10, and the devil that deceived them was cast into the lake of fire and brimstone, where the beast and the false prophet are and shall be tormented day and night forever and ever.

A covenant took place on the Cross. A covenant is a formal binding agreement or pledge between two parties. It is like a contract, but while a contract is a legal agreement involving specific terms and requirements, a covenant is a "LIFE AGREEMENT" in which the parties pledge themselves to one another, such as a marriage. In the case of God's covenant with His people, he pledges to be their

God and for them (us) to be His people. It is also like a last will and testament, "a will is in force only when somebody has died. Jesus died and was buried; He rose on the third day with power and authority to give us new life (1st Corinthians 15:3-4). The old covenant was not put into effect without the blood. There was a need for atonement, which means, 'to cover over", reparation or expiation for sin. Moses set up the old covenant by sacrificing animals and sprinkling their blood on everything connected to the covenant. Without atonement for their sins, the people of Israel would have suffered God's judgment. The reconciliation of God and humankind was made through Jesus Christ. Jesus is the one who initiates and establishes the new covenant or testament, and His ministry is far superior to the ministry of Old Testament priests, higher than the Levite priests because He belongs to a permanent priesthood that is "holy, blameless, pure, set apart from sinners, exalted above the heavens." He instituted a new covenant far superior to the old one, which is why there is no forgiveness without the shedding of blood. Sacrificing a life binds a covenant and enforces it.

Two powerful forces came together through our Lord and Savior, "The Cross and His Blood"! He was the blood sacrifice on the cross; He is the high priest using His blood to cover our sins before God. The Bible tells us in 1st John 5:8 that There are three that bear witness on earth: the spirit, water, and blood. This is a good place to stop and praise God; we do not have to kill animals as a sacrifice for our sins today because the ultimate sacrifice has been made through Jesus Christ, and there is no more sacrifice to be made. I hear the words of this song in my spirit, "one day, when I was lost, Jesus died upon the cross, and I know it was the blood for me. He hung His head and died, He hung His head and died, He hung His head and died for me, one day when I was lost, He died upon the cross, and I know it was the blood for me". I don't know about you, but I was lost. Now I'm found, and He's coming back for me. Will you be ready? Do you have Assurance of Salvation? Do you not know you are a beneficiary of the cross of Jesus? The Cross of Jesus made you a beneficiary to receive The Benefits of the Cross. Glory to God!

Every Christian desires Assurance of Salvation, the certainty that when Christ returns or death comes, they will be with the Lord Jesus in heaven. For us to know that we are in an authentic saving relationship with Jesus Christ, here are some ways to know this by the writing of Apostle John:

1)   We have the assurance of eternal life if we submit to Jesus as Lord, the supreme authority and Leader of our lives, and are sincerely trying to live by His principles and obey His commands. 1st John 2:4-5, He that saith, I know Him and keepeth not His commandments is a liar, and the truth is not in him. But whosoever keepeth His word, in

him verily is the love of God perfected; hereby know we, that we are in Him.

2)   We have the assurance of eternal life if we consistently and persistently do what is right by God's standards. 1st John 2:29: If you know that He is righteous, you know that everyone who does righteousness is born of Him.

3)   We have the assurance of eternal life if we are conscious of the Holy Spirit living within us. 1st John 3:24, And hereby we know that He abideth in us, by the Spirit which He hath given us. 1st John 4:13, Hereby we know that we dwell in Him, and He in us, because he hath given us His Spirit.

4)   We have the assurance of eternal life if we have a sincere and deep desire and steadfast hope in Christ's return; the Word of God tells us in 1st John 3:2-3, Beloved, now are we the sons of God and it doth not yet appear what we shall be; but we know that, when He shall appear, we shall be like Him; for we shall see Him as He is. And every man that hath this hope in Him purifieth himself, even as He is pure.

5)   We have the assurance of eternal life if we believe, accept, and remain in right relation to the "Word of Life"—Jesus Christ.

THE LAST SAYING OF JESUS

Jesus' Seven Last Saying on the Cross.

1)   Father forgive them; for they know not what they do--Luke 23:34

(a)   Words of forgiveness

2)   Today shalt thou be with Me in paradise--Luke 23:43

(b)   Words of Salvation

3)   Woman, behold thy son! Then saith Jesus to the disciple, Behold thy mother! Luke 19:26

(c)   Words of Love and Care

4)   My God, My God, why hast Thou forsaken Me? Mark 15:34

(d)   Words of spiritual suffering

5)   I thirst—John 19:28
(e)   Words of physical suffering

6)   It is Finished-John 19:30
(f)   Words of Triumph

7)   Father, unto Thy hands I commend My Spirit—Luke 23:46
(g)   Words of Devotion and Trust

These last seven statements of Jesus taught us about His character, faithfulness, and obedience to His Father, Love, Trust, Devotion, Commitment, Humility, and Sacrifice.

SUMMARY

Summary of "The Benefits of The Cross of Jesus".
Make the Cross personal in your life.

1)   What did the Cross do for You? Your debt has been satisfied completely.

2)   What did the Cross do to You? A divine exchange, you were made whole in Christ Jesus.

3)   Jesus Christ's death on the cross cleanses us and frees us from sin (Matthew 26:28; 1 Peter 2:24).

4)   Jesus Christ's death on the cross delivered us from God's wrath (Romans 5:9).

5)   God redeems and forgives us through Jesus Christ's death on the cross (Colossians 1:14).

6)   The death of Jesus Christ on the cross breaks Satan's power (Colossians 2:14-15; Hebrews 2:14-15).

7)   The death of Jesus Christ on the cross brings physical healing (Isaiah 53:5).

8)   The death of Jesus Christ on the cross reconciles us to God and to people (Ephesians 1:7; Ephesians 2:11-22; Colossians 1:13-20).

9)   The death of Jesus Christ on the cross gives us access to God (Hebrews 10:19-20).

10)   The death of Jesus Christ on the cross, He tastes death for everyone (Hebrews 2:9).

Jesus came to give His life as a ransom for many; He has borne the guilt of our sins, He has endured the punishment of our hell, and the justice of God has been satisfied in Him.

The Son of God wrapped himself in human flesh and became a man to live the life you and I would have to live in order to enter heaven. He came not to abolish the law but to fulfill it (Matthew 5:17). Every commandment of God was fulfilled in the life of the Lord Jesus Christ. Jesus' perfect life of obedience was now about to come to an end. The night before He died, He was able to say to His Father, "I have glorified thee on the earth: I have finished the work which thou gavest me to do. And now, O Father, glorify thou me with thine own self with the glory which I had with thee before the world was" (John 17:4-5).

The life of Jesus was a life of suffering; it was a life of obedience, but it was also a life of conflict with our enemy, the devil. The story of this conflict goes back to the beginning of the bible. Satan tempted the woman and the man and led them into sin, which caused them to lose the paradise of God. They got the knowledge of evil and came under the power of the evil one. That's been our story ever since. It is the explanation of what we see in the world today. But God promised that a Redeemer would come, saying to Satan, "You will bite his heel, but He will crush your head', this is the prophecy of a spiritual conflict between the woman's offspring, that is, the Lord Jesus Christ (Genesis 3:15). God's promise in Eden is precisely what happened at the cross. In Christ's death, He broke the devil's power. When Jesus died, He went beyond the reach of Satan. He could no longer tempt Jesus. The devil could no longer afflict Him or cause Him to suffer.

The apostle John described how someone held up a sponge soaked in vinegar on a stick, and when Jesus received the drink, He said, "It is finished." We needed a Savior who triumphed over suffering. He was plunged into indescribable suffering but was not overcome by it. He came through it and triumphed in it. That is what we have in Jesus. This was the end of His excruciating suffering. He knows suffering more than anyone has ever known it and is now seated at the right hand of the Father, where He intercedes for us.

What can be added to Jesus's redemptive work, His death, and resurrection? Absolutely Nothing! It is finished! His long-suffering is over; He's no longer on the cross. The entire course of obedience is over, and the decisive battle with His enemy is over. Christ finished, you and I haven't, but with Jesus, you will finish strong! Remember, this race that we're in for Christ is not given to the swift nor to the strongest but to the one who endures to the end. James 1:12: Blessed is the man that endureth temptation, for when he is tried, he shall receive the crown of Life, which the Lord hath promised to them that love Him. Do not forfeit your Crown of Eternal Life with the Lord Jesus Christ.

The most powerful, undeniable, unselfish act is Love went to the Cross for all humanity, for all times, all generations, and there is no greater act than the Love of Jesus Christ, our Lord, our Savior, our Master, and our Redeemer. We give God all the glory, Amen.

So, I leave you with this Psalm of David, entitled: THE BENEFITS OF THE LORD.

THE BENEFITS
OF THE LORD

Psalm 103

Bless the LORD, O my soul and all that is within me, bless his holy name. Bless the LORD, O my soul, and forget not all his benefits: who forgiveth all thine iniquities; who healeth all thine diseases; who redeemeth thy life from destruction; who crowneth thee with lovingkindness and tender mercies; who satisfieth thy mouth with good things; so that thy youth is renewed like the eagle's. The LORD executeth righteousness and judgment for all that are oppressed. He made known his ways unto Moses, his acts unto the children of Israel. The LORD is merciful and gracious, slow to anger and plenteous in mercy. He will not always chide neither will he keep his anger forever. He hath not dealt with us after our sins nor rewarded us according to our iniquities. For as the heaven is high above the earth, so great is his mercy toward them that fear him. As far as the east is from the west, so far hath he removed our transgressions from us. Like as a father pitieth his children, so the LORD pitieth them that fear him. For he knoweth our frame; he remembereth that we are dust. As for man, his days are as grass: as a flower of the field, so he flourisheth. For the wind passeth over it, and it is gone, and the place thereof shall know it no more. But the mercy of the LORD is from everlasting to everlasting upon them that fear him and his righteousness unto children's children; to such as keep his covenant and to those that remember his commandments to do them. The LORD hath prepared his throne in the heavens, and his kingdom ruleth over all. Bless the LORD, ye his angels that excel in strength, that do his commandments, hearkening unto the voice of his word. Bless ye the LORD, all ye his hosts; ye ministers of his, that do his pleasure. Bless the LORD, all his works in all places of his dominion; bless the LORD, O my soul.

ABOUT THE AUTHOR

Annette Stanley was born and raised in Kingsland, Georgia, to Mr. Curtis Way and Mrs. Madeline Way. She is a mother of three children and a grandmother of seven grandsons. She began her journey with the Lord on July 19, 2001, when she surrendered her life to the Lord. February 14, 2013, the Lord spoke to Annette's heart and said, "Preach my gospel; what a Valentine's Day present she received. Months later, she answered the call, and today, she is an ordained chosen vessel of God to preach the gospel of Jesus Christ. Annette serves under the leadership of Apostle Alva Harris and Pastor Ida Harris of Deliverance Temple in Jacksonville, Florida.